TREASURE HUNTING TOOLS

BY

Michael Mosley

I dedicate this book to all the folks in the world who seek for treasure in one form or another.

I hope that this book will serve to entertain and inform the reader about the tools and equipment that is used by treasure hunters. I hope that it will inspire the reader to go out into the world and seek for Treasure. Good luck and God bless.

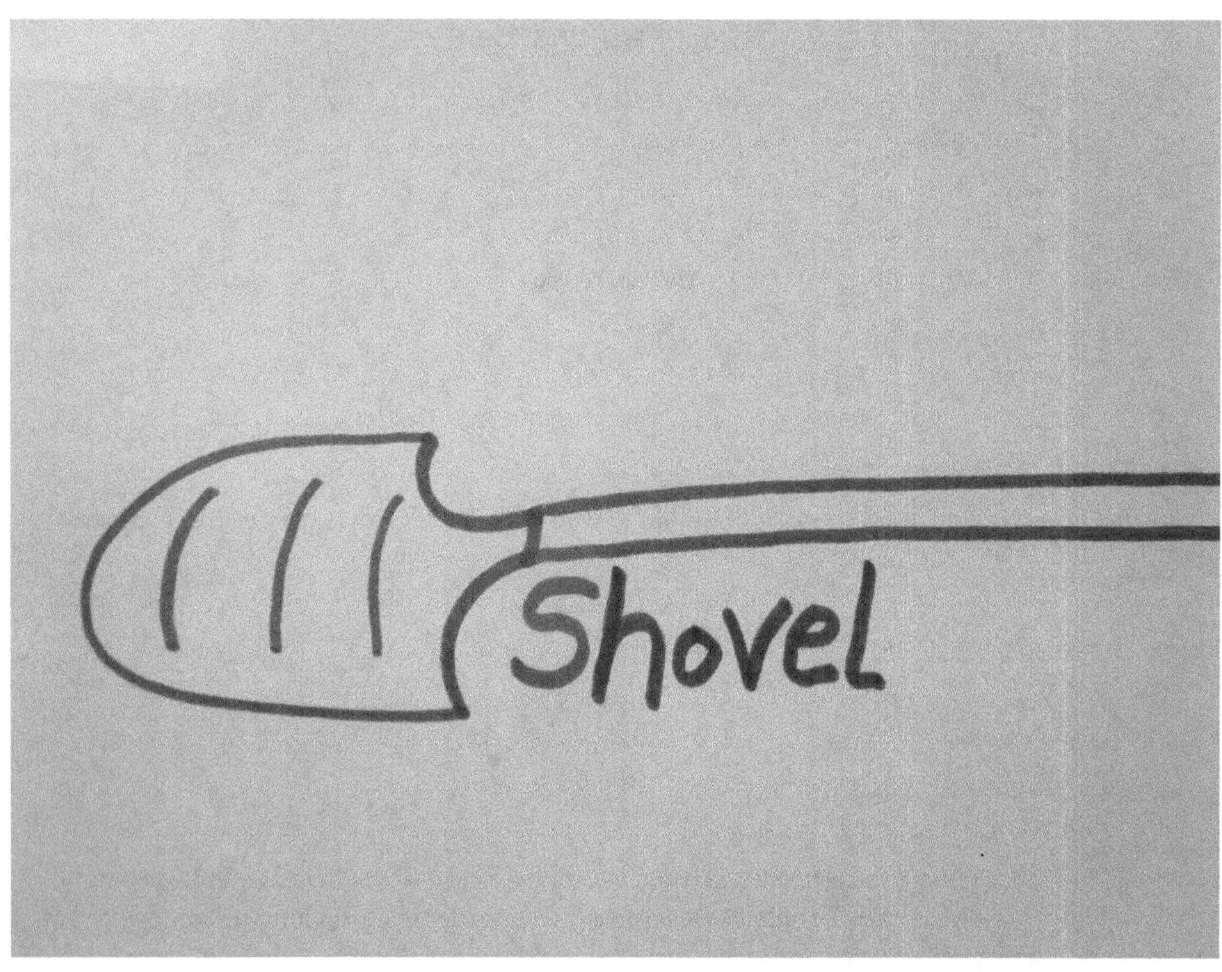

For many centuries before the Metal detector was invented, people searched for treasure by going to a site and digging in the ground at spots where they felt that treasure could have been buried in the ground. This treasure hunting was a hit-and-miss situation, but sometimes folks got lucky and found treasure. Modern day treasure hunters still need to dig up any underground items that they locate with a metal detector or dowsing rod. There are different types of shovels being manufactured and each type will come in handy for certain tasks. Small-bladed shovels, large-bladed shovels and spades, and a few other types are in use by treasure hunters today.

When searching for coins and jewelry on a beach, one of the handiest tools that you can use is a handheld sand scoop. It makes recovering small items in the sand much easier. I have had to re-dig my holes several times on many occasions because I wasn't using a sand scoop. With a sand scoop, you would rarely need to dig more than one or two times to recover the item or items. Sand scoops come in handheld versions and in versions with a long handle attached. I prefer to use one of the long handle versions because it doesn't require bending over so much as you search.

Electronic probes can be used to locate small metal items in a hole that may be difficult to locate without the electronic probe. I have never owned one of these devices, but many people use them to good effect and wouldn't go out metal detecting without one. Before these devices were invented, folks would use a coin probe to push into the ground to locate a coin or other object in the ground before digging it up. Some would actually "Pop" a coin up to the surface using a screwdriver for a probe. The head of the screwdriver was usually ground off o a round point so that it would be less-damaging to the object being recovered. The electronic probe operates off a battery or batteries and is just a device that pinpoints the item in the hole. Some folks call it a pinpointer.

A sifter is a handy tool to use to recover small items from sand, dirt, and debris. It is basically a frame with a wire or plastic screen attached to the bottom. The frame can be made of wooden boards or metal. On a sifter frame made of wood, you can attach the wire or plastic screen to the bottom with strips of wood nailed down. To use a sifter, simply throw sand, dirt, or other materials into the sifter and shake it vigorously to sift out the debris. Then inspect the items left in the screen to see if anything good has been found.

Gold prospectors use sluice boxes to more effectively find gold. They put the sluice box in a stream and the water washes out the debris and the gold gets trapped by the riffles. Sometimes carpet is used to trap gold in a sluice box. It is a much more efficient way to recover gold than a gold pan.

A metal detector is a very important tool for a treasure hunter. It can find items underground such as coins, jewelry, tokens, and many other things made of metal. Metal detectors can be set to discriminate undesirable targets and to only find desirable targets. Many buried treasures have been found by folks using a metal detector over the years since they were first invented. Metal detectors can detect gold, silver, copper, and any metal object.

A floating sifter is a good tool to use while detecting in calm water. It is basically like a regular sifter, except that it is floated on the water by some type of flotation such as pool noodles, Styrofoam bats, PVC pipes, or even plastic soda bottles. I have made a few different sifters over the years. To use a floating sifter, just throw the debris out of your scoop and the water will wash the debris out and you simply inspect the screen to see what is left behind. Most floating sifters are about 18" by 18" in size, but I have made one about 20" by 24" that I used to float across a deep creek to get to the other side where a shallower swim area was located. I even had my scoop on it with me.

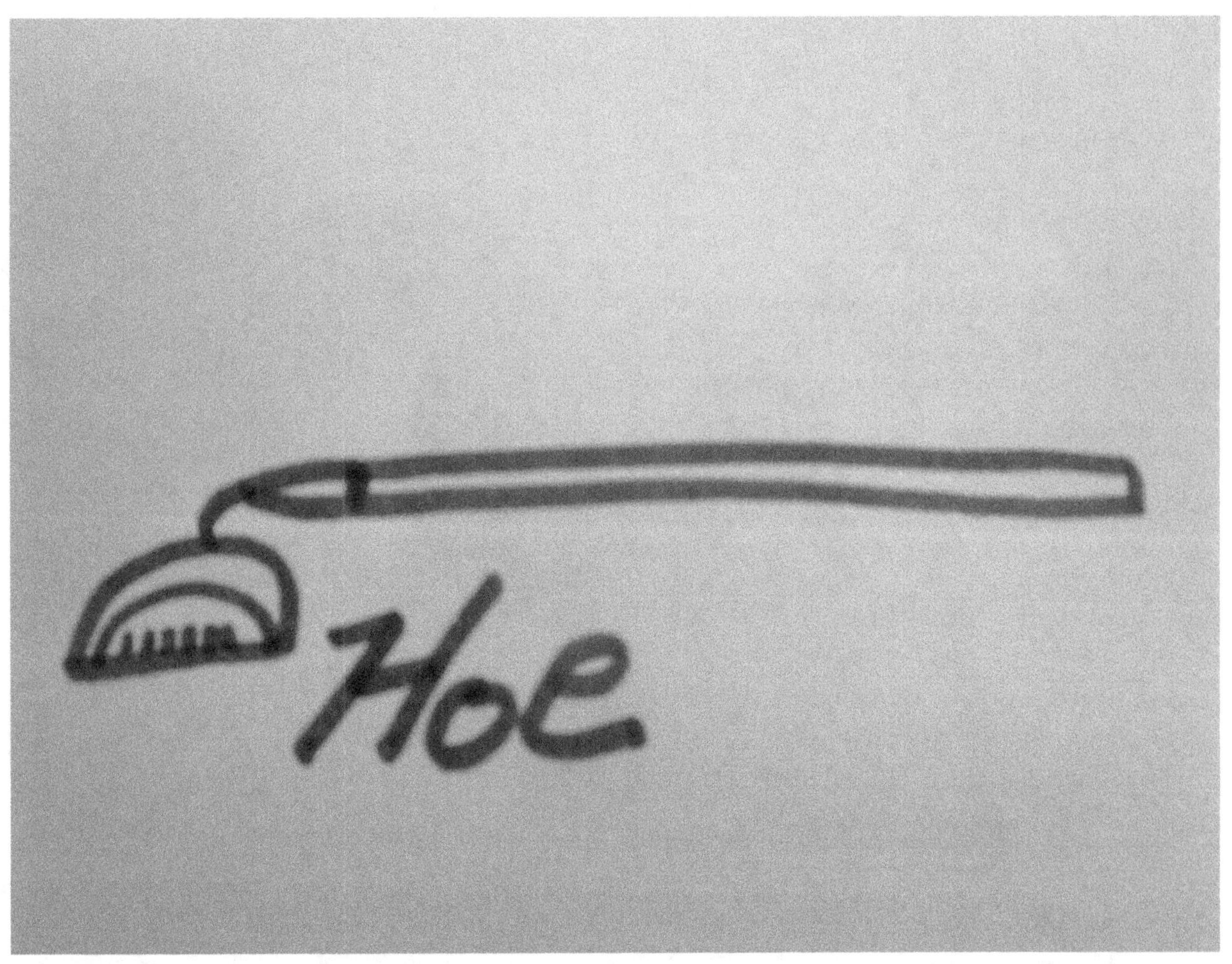

A regular garden hoe can be an effective tool to use when searching in sand and muck. In the mud of a Bay or river edge, it is a good scraping tool or chopping tool. Just chop down into the muck and pull it back toward you to uncover items.

Back before the creation of electronic probes (Pinpointers) a person would sometimes use a handheld probe that was essentially a rod attached to some type of handle. Manufacturers made them and sold them, but many people modified a screwdriver to be used as a probe. They would grind the point down to a round point so that it wouldn't be as damaging to the object being recovered. And a favorite trick of probe users was to "Pop" a coin out of the soil by placing the head of the probe under a coin and then pushing down on the handle swiftly so that the coin would pop up to the surface and out of the ground.

A long-handled beach scoop comes in very handy for water hunting. You wade along until you hear a target and then you position the scoop behind where you heard the sound. Then you push the scoop bucket into the bottom with your foot while leaning the long handle forward. Then you pull the handle back and then lift the bucket from the bottom and shake it back and forth vigorously. Then when all the debris such as dirt or sand has been washed out, you look inside the bucket and pick up the good finds and discard the trash targets (Preferably in a discard pouch or Goody Bag). Using a long-handled scoop can take getting used to and a little practice is necessary at first. But after a little use, you will have no problem with it. Long-handled scoops come with smaller holes 3/8th inch or ½" or larger 5/8th inch holes.? The 5/8th inch holes make it easier and faster to sift the debris out. The smaller 3/8th holes are able to retain smaller items such as ear ring studs, etc. I prefer the 5/8th inch size holes, because of the ease of sifting debris and sand out. The size of the holes is strictly a matter of preference.

A treasure pouch is good to have when treasure hunting with a metal detector. When you find a good item, place it in the pouch on the side designated for the keepers and when you find a junk item simply toss it into the side of the pouch designated to be discards. Manufacturers manufacture pouches for detectorists, but many people have used a simple nail apron from a hardware store. They may or may not write designations for the trash side or keeper side of the nail apron with a marker of some type. I have had to stop at a garbage can more than once on a beach hunt to throw the junk items into the can so that I wouldn't have to carry the weight of all the junk around with me as I searched.

A sturdy hand trowel comes in handy to dig up and recover items from the soil. In parks, a shovel may not be allowed or even be practical. A hand trowel is much easier to tote around and could be all that is needed to recover rings and coins at a park, etc. Trowels are made of plastic, stainless-steel, and other materials. I prefer the stainless-steel versions because they are very durable. A plastic trowel can be used for recovering items in beach sand and dirt, but the stainless-steel trowels are the most preferred by treasure hunting detectorists.

A plumbob is used by dowsers who claim to be able to locate valuables from afar. Map dowsing is a

Tool that dowsers use to locate where valuables are supposed to be hidden or buried. I have no proof

Of the validity of such a tool as a plumbob. But, some folks swear that map dowsing with a handheld

Plumbob held aloft by a string above a map can actually be used to locate valuables or other things.

A pair of tweezers can be used to pick up teeny tiny bits of gold in small crevices. Many prospectors Have used a pair of tweezers to pick up gold flakes or very small nuggets lodged in-between small crevices. And whenever stuck by a splinter, they come in handy to remove the splinter as well.

A gold pan comes in handy to recover gold from a stream in gold-bearing areas of the country. Debris are placed into the pan and then the pan is placed into a stream and the pan is moved back and forth to wash the debris out gently. When the last of the debris are washed from the pan, you inspect the bottom of the pan to see if any flakes or nuggets are there. If there is presence of gold, a dropper can be used to suck it up, or a pair of tweezers can be used to recover it from the pan. Modern- day gold pans are typically made of plastic, but back in the early days of gold panning, they were made of metal. I've read about folks back in the 1840's who would get up in the morning and cook breakfast in a frying pan, then they would begin to use the same pan to pan for gold.

A miner's pick is used to pick at the wall of a cave or the surface rock of an area. Prospectors and gemstone hunters use these picks to recover the treasure of their choice. Some folks use the picks to gather ore samples of silver, gold, and gemstones, etc.

A small-diameter search coil can be used more effectively in trashy ground that has a lot of trash targets in it such as foil, pull-tabs, nails, and other items that are of no use to a metal detectorist. The smaller size of the coil allows it to work easier in-between the trash targets to essentially cherry pick the good items from amongst the junk items. A larger search coil would be reading several junk items as one item and would confuse the detector. But the smaller-sized coil can be very effective in these areas. Many good finds have been made by detectorists who were using a small-sized search coil. The smaller size means less depth ability, but sometimes depth isn't the most desired ability of a search coil. Being able to work in very trashy areas of ground, is much more desirable in most cases.

Large-diameter search coils are best for searching ground that isn't too trash infested. Large search coils can go deeper in the ground than small-diameter search coils can. Large-diameter search coils will cover more area as a person searches with them. They are not very good for searching ground infested with lots of trash targets, because the large coil will pick up the signal from several trash targets at once and confuse the detector. For trashy ground, a smaller-sized coil is best. For cache hunting and relic hunting, a large coil is preferred by most folks.

Metal detectors run off of batteries. The 2 most common types of batteries used in metal detectors, are 9v batteries and AA batteries. Usually a detector running on 9v batteries will use from 1 to 4 batteries. And detectors using AA batteries use from 2 to 8 batteries. Now, of course there are some exceptions to this information. I've heard of detectors that run off of 12 to 16 AA batteries. And there are detectors that run off different batteries than 9V or AA batteries. Some older detectors run off C batteries. And some detectors run off of rechargeable battery packs. Especially some of the underwater machines.

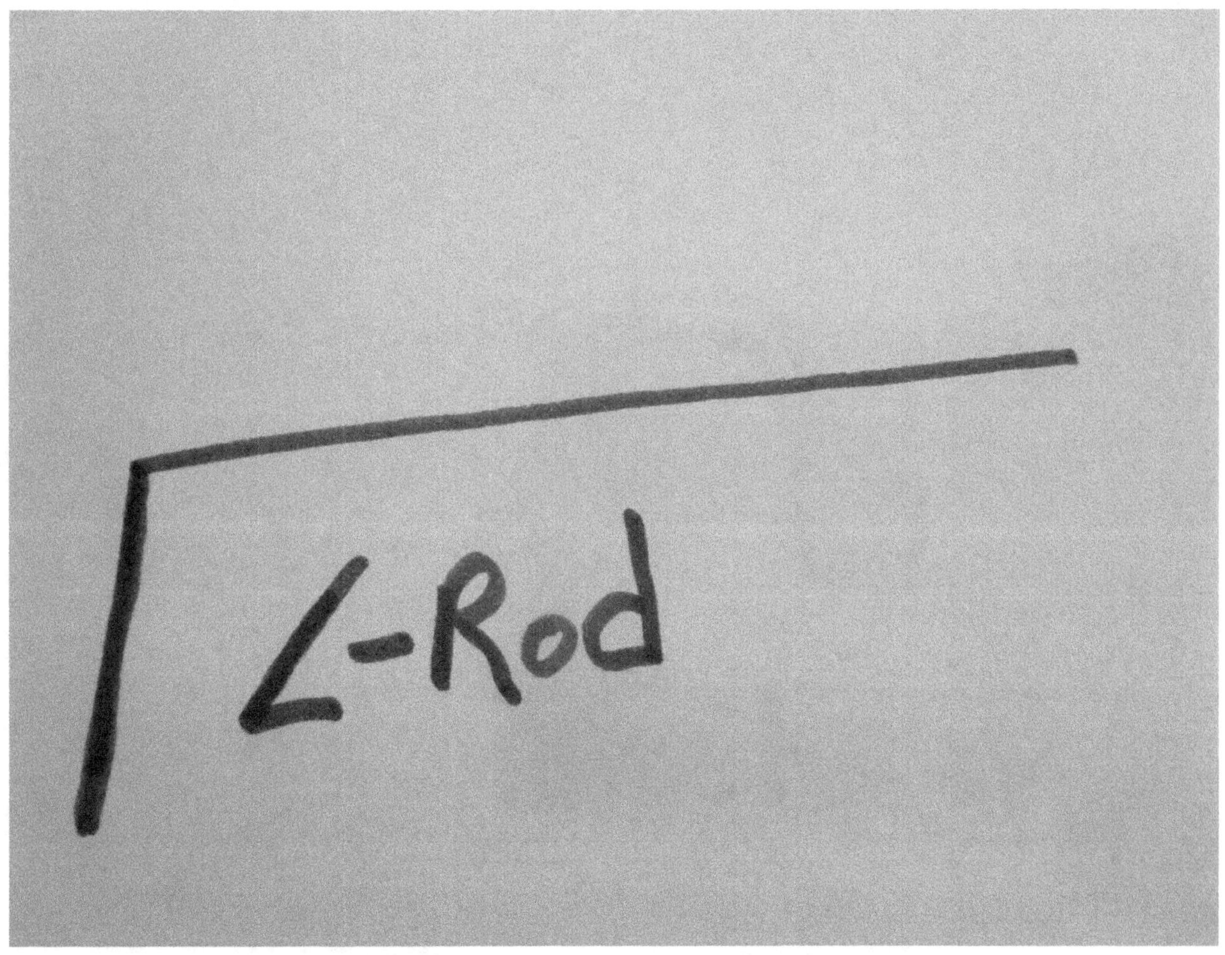

L-Rods are simply rods bent into the shape of an L and are used by dowsers to locate items such as silver and gold, etc. Some people claim to be able to locate treasures with them. Some folks claim to be able to locate underground tunnels and such with them also. I know that they can help you locate a underground pipe or a metal object such as a buried can, etc. I have experimented with one a few of them and can locate a water pipe or some such item under the ground with one. In Vietnam, soldiers even located land mines with them. Some folks claim to be able to locate missing people with them also.

Headphones are very important to metal detectorists. A person wearing headphones can hear the deeper quieter signals that wouldn't be heard as well without headphones. At the beach, a pair of headphones can make it possible to hear the signals when loud waves are crashing on the beach. And headphones will allow a person to be more discreet with their detecting. Folks get more nosey whenever they hear the loud sound of a detector sounding out. I'd rather not get everyone's attention when I'm trying to metal detect a site. A volume control comes as a standard feature of most headphones. And audio-enhancing ability is available for folks who have hearing impairments.

The Treasure Hunter's Code of ethics is basically to get permission to search and always leave a

site in as good a condition as it was when you began your search. Cover up all your excavations.

Respect the land owner's property. Respect and listen to the instructions given to you by the land

owner. Do to them and theirs as you would have them do unto you. Be a good steward of the hobby.

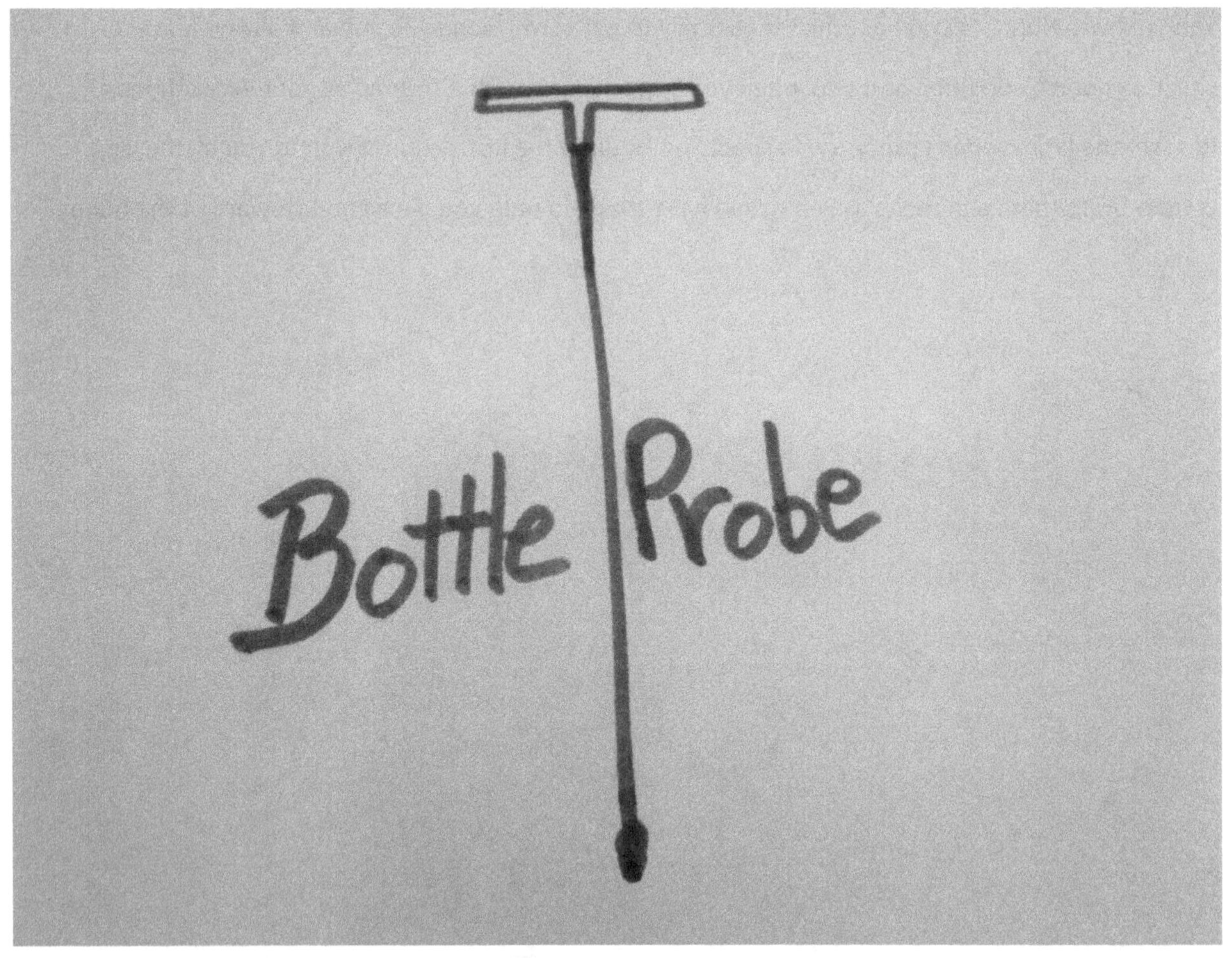

A bottle probe is a tool that is used to find bottles in the ground. It is a length of rod with a tip on one end and a handle of some kind on the other end. I've seen them with T handles and with a round ball or doorknob for a handle. The probe is basically pushed into the ground and if it strikes a glass object such as a bottle or a crockery jug, etc. It will make a certain sound. An experienced user will be able to tell if it has hit something made of glass or something else. Probes are made by manufacturers in different lengths. Of course, many people make their own probes out of antennas and even rods that come out of old cars, etc. The tip usually has a special shape that allows the probe to be pushed into the ground easy and then withdrawn from the soil easily.

A scratcher is a simple garden tool that people use to scratch in the soil of a flower garden with. A bottle digger uses a scratcher to scratch out the debris that surrounds the bottles in an old bottle dump, etc. The glass bottles are usually brittle and can fracture or break in-two when pressure is put on them. A plastic or nylon scratcher is used to gently scratch away the dirt and other debris that surround the bottles. Most folks put a broom handle into the back of it (The scratcher usually has a plug in the end that can come out to put a handle in).

Scratcher